what the fortune teller didn't say

What
the
Fortune
Teller
Didn't
Say

by Shirley Geok-lin Lim

West End Press

Some of these poems have appeared in the following anthologies and collections: *Bridges: Literature Across Cultures* (1993); *Flinders Jubilee Anthology* (1991); *From the Listening Place: Languages of Intuition* (1997); *Imagining Worlds* (1994); *Into the Nineties: Post-Colonial Women's Writing* (1994); *Literary Olympians, 1992* (1992); *On Prejudice: A Global Perspective* (1993); *Premonitions* (1995); *Southeast Asia Writes Back!* (1993); *The Pen is Mightier than the Sword* (1994); *Unsettling America: An Anthology of Contemporary Multicultural Poetry* (1994); *Westerly Looks to Asia* (1993).

Some of these poems have appeared in the following journals: *Feminist Studies, Literary Review, Massachusetts Review, New Straits Times, Poetry Review, River Styx, Shantih, Solidarity,* and *Tampa Review*.

First edition, September 1998
ISBN 0-931122-91-0

Book design by Nancy Woodard
Front cover from the painting *Woman of Colors* by Joanna L. Kao.

Distributed by University of New Mexico Press

West End Press • PO Box 27334 • Albuquerque, NM 87125

For Blair Hull, whose endowment of the Hull Chair in Women's Studies at the University of California, Santa Barbara, testifies to his lasting commitment to support women, social justice, and human rights.

Contents

what the fortune teller didn't say

What the fortune teller didn't say

When the old man and his crow
picked the long folded parchment
to tell my fortune at five,
they never told about leaving,
the burning tarmac and giant wheels.
Or arriving—why immigrants
fear the malice of citizens
and dull shutterings of those
who hate you whatever you do.

My mother did not grip
my hand more possessively.
Did I cry and was it corn
ice-cream she fed me because
the bird foretold a husband?
Wedded to unhappiness,
she knew I would make it,
meaning money, a Mercedes
and men. She saw them shining

in the tropical mildew
that greened the corner alley
where the blind man and his
moulting crow squatted
promising my five-year-old hand
this future. Of large faith
she thrust a practical note
into the bamboo container,
a shiny brown cyclinder
I wanted for myself, for
a cage for field crickets.

With this fortune my mother bought,
only the husband is present,
white as a peeled root, furry
with good intentions, his big nose
smelling a scam. Sometimes,
living with him, like that
black silent crow I shake
the cylinder of memory
and tell my fortune all over again.
My mother returns, bearing
the bamboo that we will fill
with green singing crickets.

Hands

My mother taught me.
Use right hand to mix rice and *sambal*,
cool white paste and blistering chilies
so fresh they burn the tongue like shame.
Use left hand to wipe the backside,
thick yellow paper squares we cut
once a week for cleaning ourselves.
Two hands to serve tea,
thumbs behind, fingers curled,
in a ring of obedience.

My mother wasn't

I.
My mother was *Chye Neo,*
Chinese; cursed fate that
married her at sixteen,
a good eldest daughter
who kept secrets of *Nonya*
dishes. Before I could learn
how to grind milled rice
to paste for unwrinkling
the wickedest face,
to plump palm-leaf cups
with yeasty rice and sugar
for fermenting cakes
that ladies eat, drunk,
roisterous through afternoons;
before I could learn why
she cried after the sixth babe
was born, why she lost
her gold bangles, and why
I was a daughter
not a son, she left.
I never found her again.
I never found the unbroken
vessel of childhood.

II.
In my dream my mother comes to me,
saying, I have forgiven you.
I am angry—who gives you
the right to forgive me? I don't want
forgiveness. Take back your love
you give without asking,

without a price to it. Take back
your forgiveness. No one who gives
away her daughter has a right
to love her. I will not forgive you
till I have made you pay the full
debt of your abandonment.

III.
My mother is sleeping.
For once she isn't gazing at me.
Her chubby unhealthy cheeks glow
with a greed for life.
Her little nose snores like
a piglet after its first milk meal.
I watch my mother sleeping
at the teat of the full world
she has always wanted.
Her hair is thin; pale bald patches
glisten like an older man
she would have given me to
had she thought about what she was doing.
Pariah on the pandan mat,
like herself fifty years ago,
a fat child trained for marriage,
given over to the market.
I look at her with an enemy's eye,
my mother, my purveyer,
who repeats in her sleep the innocence
of daughters preparing for the cruel night.
In her sleep, I am the sow
preparing to eat my young.

Mother's shoes

In my mother's shoes I was short
of imagination, stuffed full of
ancestors, recessive genes.
Mother wanted fine things, confused
life with wanting, carried in
from the P & O steamboats smoking
off Malacca godowns. No Asian
bazaar, but the latest
Western fashions: Elizabeth Arden,
Max Factor, Jantzen, Christian Dior.
She wanted dollars repeating
in a dozen furnished rooms. Limos
of German muscle, triple-spray-
painted, airconditioned, leather
upholstery, permanent, sealed-
in-plastic: one for her, one for me,
and one for show. No hot taxis
for mother, fumbling for small
change, airs, from a creaky purse.
Mother was a forward-looking
lady, wanted a good perm, curls
like the British *mems* buying
at Cold Storage. She didn't know
what her hair looked like until
it began to fall out.
                    I've kicked off
mother's shoes (mother, mother,
crying late alone), damned the dreams
of poor young women: no more
stepping into mother's fashion shoes.

At the funeral parlors, Singapore Casket Company

Perhaps the past is a paper house. —Patricia Ikeda

Pastor John in platform shoes walks to the boom
box on the concrete floor, bends down and turns
the knob till the volume hisses, "WE SHALL
MEET BY THAT BEAUTIFUL SHORE." Red-hot
ginger blossoms gape among maiden-hair fern,
their musk jabbing like carrion.
A pale lemon giant worm, you lie embowered
beneath more bouquets than lovers or children
had delivered to your door. "What honor!"
someone whispers of the calling cards
from the corporate brother's rich associations.
They fall off frangipani leis, names engraved
like so many gold-rimmed kinfolk.
This moment is new. Disbelief lies
on your waxy cheek. Before the sermon
Pastor John invites a prophetic bond with me,
the daughter from New York. I have arrived
decades late, after the red Singapore-
chopped aerogrammes that urged Scripture
and held out for attention.
                    Then the charismatics
are gone: the Chinese pastor headed for Los Angeles,
greying ladies and lonely Tamil adolescents,
minor bureaucrats whose Christ raises the dead,
who are looking for nothing your island can offer.

I also leave you, to gawk at the Taoist shaman.
He stacks pyramids of gold paper bricks
before the Chinese funeral room next door.
I watch for his unknown dead as he
pours brandy over the extravagant wealth
and sets the conflagration with a Cricket
barbecue starter. Electric blue Mercedes
models and towering skyscrapers
flash up behind acetate Maytag deep freezers.
The black-hatted paper man in coattails
toasts crisply down to a twisted heap.
Casually the Taoist jumps over the fire, once, twice,
three times. Lifting black robes above his pants
he clears the flames. The bamboo scaffolds burn slower,
glowing after the papery ash collapses,
after you have been delivered
to the crematorium accompanying
Christian smoke and ash into the earth.

Starlight Haven

Susie Wong was at the Starlight Haven,
the Good Times Bar and Sailors Home.
It was always dark at noon:
you had to blink three times before
you could see Susie standing by
the washed chutney jar half-filled
with ten and twenty-cent coins.
When the bar was empty her eyes were sad
and she'd mop the formica tables,
dry a row of tall Anchor Pilsner
glasses. The wet cloth slap-slapped
like Susie's japanese slippers
over the dirty floor.
                        Then the swing-doors
bang and the darkness is full of white
uniforms, full of cold Tigers
sweating in warm air-conditioning.
I think of the flutter in Susie's pulse.
Buy a drink, Tommy boy! G. I. Joe!
Yankee Doodle! Howdy Doody! Romeo!
and suddenly Johnny Mathis
like black magic is crooning "Chances Are."
Her girlish voice is soft and happy,
soft like a tubby belly after
six babies and ten years of beat-up
marriage, happy as only Singapore
Susie Wongs can be, when Johnny
and Ray are rocking the bottles
and their tops pop off and the chutney
jar is singing chink, chink.

The red-faced brawny men are laughing
at her voice. Quack, quack, they laugh
so hard they spill Tigers over
the plastic counter. Quack, quack, fuck, fuck.
Susie looks at the bar-man who makes
his coolie eyes dumb black stones
and wipes up the yellow puddles
without a grunt.
                  Thirty years later
I hear mother singing "In the sweet
bye and bye." She is a Jesus woman
grown up from bar-girl. Sailors and Tommies
have disappeared from her Memory Lane.
I still keep the bracelet mother gave me,
gold saved from beer spilled on the clean
tables, her clean lap. I savor the taste
of that golden promise, never to love men
in white who laugh, quack, quack.

Ah Mah

Grandmother was smaller
than me at eight. Had she
been child forever?

Helpless, hopeless, chin sharp
as a knuckle, fan face
hardly half-opened, not a scrap

of fat anywhere: she tottered
in black silk, leaning on
handmaids, on two tortured

fins. At sixty, his sons all
married, grandfather bought her,
Soochow flower song girl.

Every bone in her feet
had been broken, bound tighter
than any neighbor's sweet

daughter's. Ten toes and instep
curled under, yellow petals
of chrysanthemum, wrapped

by gold cloth. He bought the young
face, small knobby breasts
he swore he'd not dress with sarong

of maternity. Each night
he held her feet in his palms,
like lotus on the tight

hollows of celestial lakes.
Against the calluses her
weightless soles, cool and slack,
clenched by his stranger's fever.

Nonya[1]

The cockle spines prick my fingers.
Ma warns, be careful passing water
in the garden. Worms, hermit crabs,
red ants bite, leave marks of possession.
So we don't bathe in the sea
at the bottom of the garden.

Ma doesn't notice the sea,
although I do and wander
down to the waves when she's not looking.

Something's in the water far out—
drowned ships, engines that make salt
like my eyes make spots after staring
in the sun too long. Of course,
ikan merah, ikan kembong,[2]
mackerel, also live in the water.
I remember this when I throw them
gutted and fresh into the curry pot.

But I'm thinking of pearls, like those
on the old queen's neck, maybe even
diamonds. Some mornings I pick crystals
in the sand and hide them under
the *beling-beling*[3] bush. The *beling-beling* fruit
is green and sour—like an old maid,
like me, ma says.

                    Yesterday
I cut the *sireh*[4] for third aunt-in-law.
She showed me the diamond on her hair-pin.
The crystals under the *beling-beling*
do not have the water in them like this—

sea squeezed hard and small. I felt
a pain break free in my chest, as if
I knew how a man must feel, slippery
as the sea and hard as its stone.

1. an assimilated Chinese Malaysian woman
2. red snapper, flounder
3. a green, sour fruit
4. betel-nut leaf

Ballad of the father

When Father sold shoes,
    my mother bought gold.
We were six children
    before they were old.
He drove a Hillman,
    was favored in town
by gamblers and nurses
    with whom he'd go down
to the small city lights.
    Mahjongg and cabaret:
these few pleasures
    composed his day.

The shop was the first to go,
    then the gold,
then Mother who saw
    all her jewelry sold.
She packed up her bruises
    for large Singapore,
for Change Alley bars,
    bazaars and stores.
He didn't shoot us,
    although we ate like rats
and outgrew our clothes
    (yet never were fat).

An ordinary kind
    in ordinary misery,
he labored to keep us
    a family.
The pity of a life:
    and nothing to add

but struggle and love
    that can make children mad.
Struggle and love
    peeling him to his core,
to a dumbness stuck,
    final, and poor.

Father in China

My father from Malaysia
stands under a tree in China
fifteen years ago. A lichee tree
in Canton's People's Park. Mr. Wer
who is also at the Clinic
takes the picture with slightly
shaking hands. It is a frugal picture,
black and white, two inches by
two inches, sent across two oceans,
creased by crazy white lines like
a cracked egg, although for fifteen years
I have preserved it in plastic
between student visas, in a succession
of wallets, between check book
and dollar notes. He is gaunt,
he who loves oyster omelets,
long noodles, pure white of pork fat
between skin and lean. Now he counts
his white blood cells, reciting
numbers in letters home as he
recited mahjongg scores a year ago.
He will not let the Malaysian
doctor cut his throat. He writes,
Chinese medicine can also
calibrate blood-cells. I am unhoused
in yet another country.
I do not know how to write
to him. I do not have his motherland
address. I do not pick up
the black coffin telephone.
No one tells me he's dead
till he's been buried.

Today I would call Canton
person-to-person. I'd say,
I've booked a ticket for you
to Sloan-Kettering. See, I have bank
accounts and dollar notes to save
your life here in another country.
Instead I write this poem.

Black and white

In my middle-aged dream
I talk to my younger father
openly, affectionately.
He's his usual pale self,
thinner than I remember
when he was a man and
I a sullen daughter.
Now he's a figure in a snapshot,
a specimen of cancer,
taken at the zoo in Guangdong.

Waking I turn to listen
to the news on television
so I don't have to remember
my dream, his mortal life.
But it persists. He is vulnerable,
come alive from the black and white
as if I have moved into
a twelve-inch sixties screen,
falling asleep on the cool linoleum
before the flashing images.

He watches American shows—
John Wayne, Bill Haley, the American
Bandstand—saying, Look! meaning,
the young kids rocking and rolling.
They're just like you!
Suddenly seeming to understand
who I was—the girl doing the twist,
the cha-cha. All night in tight blue jeans
and give-away lipstick, moving
to the drums of the conga.

That heavy Malacca night
I fell asleep in front
of his black and white television.
In my sleepiness I was
not one of those swirling skirts,
clean-bobbed hair and rolled-down socks.
My body grew black earth.
Rubbing my elbow creases
I made small dirt balls appear
like opium shit.

Dipped in permanent chemicals,
my hair frizzed, refused to bloom.
Between my legs a dangerous charm
I never showed my father.
A feather talisman,
an inkling of my future.
So he thought me black and white,
like an American, his *Peranakan*[1]
daughter, who has tamed
her dancing body, till in my dream

she is only a child. Affectionate,
open, she talks to her father
about love—his power to hold
his children in his power. No secrets
about my love for him now,
for in my memory he is disappearing,
pound for pound, into the photograph
of a man, hardly middle-aged,
with his good-bye smile, and I want
to weep, to hold his body for once,
as a woman holds a child,
so that her caring may be cleansed.

1. native-born

Father from Asia

Father, you turn your hands toward me.
Large cracked bowls, they are empty
stigmata of poverty. Light pours
through them, and I must back away,
for you are dangerous, father
of poverty, father of ten children,
father of nothing, from whose life
I have learned nothing for myself.
You are the father of childhood,
father from Asia, father of sacrifice.
I renounce you, keep you in my sleep,
keep you two oceans away. Ghost
who eats his own children, father
who lives at the center of the world,
Whose life I dare not remember,
for memory is a wheel that crushes,
and Asia is dust, is dust.

Watching

She has nothing to give.
She is not screaming. Her body screams.
I am watching her.

She is fat muscle ugly. Mother stands
common stone. She hates this man.
They have nothing to give each other.

She glares, has had it. Enough!
Out with him, the present, the past, the children.
I am watching them.

He is angry, blazing, a mean fire.
But he laughs, he can't be sad, burns, leaving
the stone fired hard: nothing to give.

He hits, he hits, he raises his fist.
Draws blood, blue green purple cuts open
the skin. I am watching them.

She bled, a stone drawn in blood.
Mother dead, father dead.
They had nothing to give.
I am watching still.

Listening to the Punjabi singer

Her Urdu voice rises in the performance room.
I could have been married for twenty years
to the man she's singing for—the beloved
who does not return her love and vanishes
forever. Always suffering Asia!

I yearn to be her this evening.
Suffused, securely my own woman,
I play at nostalgia, imagine—
eyes closed—Malaysia now, as if
twenty years have passed and nothing's died.

Not the dream of marriage, of one brown
family and nation. From back-of-the-room
middle age spins fantasy and regret.
Singles the concrete bungalow
in Petaling Jaya, one of thousands

of a race: Malay, Chinese, Indian,
and Eurasian hardened in the same
shelter, if not skin. In front of the white
stone an iron gate, bars, curlicues,
three-inch chain and lock. By the gate

hibiscus, oleander, jacarandas
with dirty plum blossom. Leafage I prune
with words threatens to overtake the evening,
just as the singer has overtaken,
sending me back, in a language I do not know,

to the place of colored doors, the riotous
vegetation, choices, and wild consequences.

Mango

A mango at the New York A. & P.
at eighty-nine American cents each,
heaped by apples: a stony red, puffy
hybrid all the way from Acapulco,
from corporate farms and rich Yankee
enterprises.
                  Then two days later,
Older Brother slowly drives me, Straits-born,
home through narrow, rewritten Malacca.
Before broken Chinese houses whose sons
and grandsons have left for Australia,
umbrella trees drop welcome shade.
Crescent mangoes like smooth-thighed trailer-
girls from Siam gleam among sickle-drawn
leaves.
                  I eat a green mango. Solid,
sour, it cuts the back of the throat, torn
taste, like love grown difficult or separate.
More chilies, more salt, more sugar,
more black soy—a memory of tart
unripeness sweetened by necessities.

Where do we go from here, carrying
those sad eyes under the mango trees,
with our sauces, our petty hauntings?

Jet lag
(at Subang airport)

Sometimes I wake up and do not remember
where I am. Jet lag is here and occurs
at any time. I forget for the moment
who I am. Lives long dead stir with power.
Faces, given up, return, asking recognition.

We catch the S. I. A. shuttle
to K. L., alphabet countries
grounded in colonial ironies.
Steaming face-towel heat
engorges the palms. All pricks and swells
of other lives rub like thighs
chafed against tenderest skin.
Nothing hides the toughened
malaise that feeds desire
to staleness, not the persistent
wintry hum and thump of machine-
purged oxygen nor glass expanses
like glittering zircons.

Flying into Subang, grey-ash
pilings of gashed lunar mounds
and ponds as blue as sky, filled
with inverted cloudy landscapes,
tilt navy, aqua and yellow-grey.
The new palm checkerboards bloom
prolific plantations despite
their postcolonial history.

We will never stop being overwhelmed
by history and race: what's allowed
in the gleaming airport—exhaustion
of racial home-coming.

lost name woman

The gift

At eight I become an animal.
Hunger sniffs, growls
at every corner, the dragon
stomps and dances on my poor head.

Every tree's a meal—
butterfruit pulped in
fuzzy jacket, stone guava
with gravelled core, even

tropical cherry-berries
which squish like bird-shit.

I hide in every corner
place where you can never
find me—dark under
hibiscus edge

cool by a back drain.
Crawl into my skin,
keep under cover,
listening to the quiet,

to the noisy dragon
spitting and shaking. She
and I were born together,
but I am wild.

I want to eat grass,
frangipani white
as sugar crusts,
just as the sun eats me,
melting in drops,
and licking
like a lolly.

The rebel

Tonight I will think of my uncles.
For once I will walk in their spirit,
pile mahjongg tiles in great walls
and crash them down with two big fists.
I will be reckless and roast opium
balls over spirit lamps. I will close
my eyes in fox women harems
and wake to male children,
this one with my bulbous nose,
these with staggered pointed teeth
like handsome crocodiles,
a dozen black-headed sons
to curse and gamble like me.

What fun my uncles had, springing
knives, fighting, using their
full confident voice.
This morning I sang with the car windows up,
letting my voice go its natural length.
What a revelation to hear my voice
as it is, booming in natural rhythm.
Did my uncles always speak in their voice?
Did no one tell them to be quiet,
be gentle, be soft, to whisper,
to hush? I with seven uncles
am forbidden to walk in their path.
Tonight I'll speak like my uncles,
I'll tell those who taught me to be
a girl, I'm not, not, not, not, not.

To a poet who died young
(To C.P.)

I.
Dead a quarter of a century
you have never been more alive
to me than now. Sandals sliding on dusty
feet, I walk the bleeding laterite
in search of your home. Would you have approved
the warning signs, red traffic light,
or overhead pass across dangerous
highways? Or dashed impatiently,
reckless only child, between Mercedes
and buses? Daughter of immigrants,
born between colonial and colonized,
your mother's hair spins brilliant
white in Singapore October sun.
Humped with age, she hears, politely,
half of my careful words. I want
to tell her a white butterfly flew
beside me as I stumbled the raw earth
toward your steep garden, that you
are writing yourself, still, as I read.
But I shout nothing into her good ear;
leave her standing in forgetting and sleep.

II.
Barely twenty you must have believed
you didn't have time to live. Men
worried you, that they should want
your impure youth, that you should give

yourself away just for the asking
of a pirate face or a cunning
mind. Born in Malacca, white among
Asians, an anxiety of belonging,

layers of oddness in your ordinary
fare, teased you to bed with strangers;
drove you to Montreux slopes to slam
down winters, and, always in a hurry,

in your screaming red car, to face
the wet night roads. You did not wait
for time, our slow lover, to show the way,
the difficult way, between race and race.

III.
This is what I would like to believe:
you stood watch as I flew through the door
like a moth in the warm night, limp,
unconscious. Death was beside me,
waiting to take me to the dark water,
skin clammy with dew, blood in my hair.
My flesh he had eaten in sheets;
but my mind fled before him in horror.
There at the place of your birth—
dear prepositional fulcrum—I broke
on the tarmac, speechless. So they kill us
for boldness, for trying, for driving
in the black night, we young women
who don't know what we want; but you,
already dead, stood beside me.
Your rapid heartbeat in protest,
you shone the lamp of intelligence
and drove the beast to his hole. I hold
your book in my live hand and read you
in words you'd dreamed up a life ago.
I believe this is what you would want.

The shape of words

The shape of words
in the mouth is thick,
like *jok*—rice, ginger, chicken stock.
In print, round yet narrow,
virgin lying flat, feet
together, precise.
In the mind, a bitter
square, peoples clashing,
not yet a holocaust.

The double

She dreamed the grand dream,
wished the million-dollar wish.
Sighed Cleopatra's heart,
claimed the heroine's part.

She tightened waist,
unbuttoned her blouse,
halfed self and parted thighs,
laughed loudly above her cries.

She smelled treachery,
worked the crowds, kissed strangers,
forgot her child, stayed up late
plotting her life. Her I hate.

Immigrant

An immigrant, she's
afraid of travelling,
stained invitation cards,
piss in the subway.
Highways shake
like clog dances,
the backroads mind
their own business,
and sidewalks grow
between air-pockets.
She dances. The landscape
of newness nauseates.
In her sleep she's lost,
wakes up, five,
under another moon.

Eating salt

I do it daily. Sleeping,
I chew handsful, dream candy.
Others sip soda pop.
Behind their backs
I lick grains, coarse
and harsh, excrement
dried from paleolithic
oceans, my fish cells
finding their way
to memorial
stormy turbulence.

Bread and cheese

With money in the bank I buy
bread and cheese for supper,
eat the slices without plate
or fork, on my narrow pension bed.
Coming into a new city
I am afraid of poverty,
I am always poor.

The cheese is unrefrigerated, sweaty.
The bread crumbles in a circle.

Bread and cheese will keep me
walking past windows full
of reflections. Coats and boots
merging into transparencies:
crystal, silver, diamonds.
My reflection also hovers,
surface among surfaces, while
in my pocket mumble
the remnants of bread and cheese.

Walking around in a different language

Every day the syllables surge like waves (oder Reise, noch nicht,
Ausgang, Dichter), a bang against your doors of perception that bar
progress.

If you listen hard enough, you could imagine yourself speaking it in
this life (Sprechen Sie Deutsch? Nein, nein. Ich spreche es nicht.)

Not the grammar in books, or on train notices,
nor the lips that open, close, smile pityingly.
But here in my mouth this round word,
a marble of my identity, rolls out, faster and faster.

Lost name woman

Mississippi China woman,
why do you wear blue jeans in the city?
Are you looking for the rich ghost
to buy you a ticket to the West?

San Francisco China woman,
you will drink only Coca-Cola.
You stir it with a long straw,
sip ss-ss like it's a rare elixir.

Massachusetts China woman,
you've cut your hair and frizzed it.
Bangs hide your stubborn brow, eyes
shine, hurricane lamps in a storm.

Arizona China woman,
now you are in Gold Mountain Country,
you speak English like the radio,
but will it let you forget your father?

Woman with the lost name,
who will feed you when you die?

White

A white hair, color
of nothing, invisible
on her brown arm, a piece
of string or twine to tie
the summer dazzle.
Only a flash of sun
renders it visible—
black gone as if never was.
Chinese black, color
of stone ink on rice-paper,
or young woman's pubic hair
coarse as telephone wires.

She hears a nuthatch
in the overgrown privet
sing, remembers the nest
beneath the overhang she'd
knocked apart last spring:
two perfect blue eggs
cradled in the straw,
among twigs and soft breast feathers,
deceptive, like the oval
fingernails of a blue baby
born perfectly dead.
Is it the same nuthatch
trying one more season?
Its whistle in the afternoon
pierces her ears with useless
desire, stripped thread
through the years' runnels.

Pensée

Between you and the obituary:
what did you say, and did it matter?
And the mortician knew your secrets finally.

I don't mind some destitution—the loneliness that refuses a hand.
An empty hour fills up like a cup at the faucet
flowing with that colorless stuff, refreshing the thirstiest mouth.

I look at women I need
as mothers, and dread their dying.
I dread all women's dying.

To be another woman is too easy.
Dreadful—that another's deprivations
should become the story you want to tell.

How long does it take for a place to enter
the blood stream, recognition to appear in dream language?
If you cannot sign it, you cannot write it.

Too old for nostalgia,
only the weeds of drift
spring overnight.
We want so hard to believe things matter.
Will someone read these words in another world?
In our world will we read them again without disillusion?

Reading book after book of poetry, loosening feeling,
aural presences, spindrifts of smoke curling above chimneys, breakers,
the wild stony hills of Yorkshire, Montana, Yunnan, Palestine.

Something matters world after world:
terra, land, earth, place
un/tongued, un/worded, blooded.

I write to eat the vinegar of blame,
and find no lie convincing, no singing word, feeling, poetry—
the same returning beat after beat after beat—none.

A knot in the brain resists a barbed wire twist,
rusted iron hammertow, tender bunion:
Pulls, flesh of flesh, against flesh.

Outside the vision box, light wavering, chlorophyll.
Water wavering, sounds dissolving, in/gather
beyond heaven, horizon and holes.

This prickly declaration ties letters like cans to rattling self.
I am, I see, I must, I will.
Threads, knots, on the long steel winding.

Presumed guilty

Born guilty, I heard the story
of two sisters—the older one
despised by the second wife, thrown
into a well to find herself in an orchard
loaded with grapefruit, the trees
like pregnant women flinging their limbs
in torment, crying, pick me, pick me.
And she did, for five years till every
green tree was stripped to anorexia.
Then entered the castle kitchen
where staggered rows of brick ovens
moaned through the brown mouths of loaves,
oh take me, take me out. She did,
the loaves so thick they tapped
like hollow heads. Five years
until the ovens gaped dark holes
emptied of mouths. Then found herself
in front of Second Mother's house,
explaining where ten years had gone,
while pearls large as rosary beads,
undimpled, rolled out with her speech,
and her feet shone in self-reflexive
calcified pools.
        Now, Second Mother,
wanting only the best for her own
warty daughter, pushed the younger,
screaming, into the smooth brown eye
of the willing well! Which blinked,
and she was walking through the same
plantation and through that steamy
torpid factory of a hundred thousand loaves.

Why bother when all she needed
was an apple to bite into
and one loaf for an afternoon's
appetite? She was out of that well
in a moment with Mother fainting
as toads jumped out each time
she told why it wasn't for her
to do the picking.
                    I had learned
one lesson, swallowing the entire
well by eight: the water of make-believe,
reproduction stories, girl slavery
redeemed by the gift of female speech,
suffering that ends in marvellous
narrative: the lie of one thrown away,
returning with a mouth that spits
what everyone—even
murderous stepmothers—desire.

learning to love america

In paradise

"Don't take the short cut,"
the girl at the front desk says,
"not when there's no school,
it's like a link trail, deserted."

She speaks the delicate power
of threat women teach daughters
and daughters' daughters.

Along a broad pavement
overgrown with frangi and mild
saffron stars I walk.

A young man exposes himself,
coughs in the green shade
like Adam in a new orchard.

Caught, I cross traffic, taking
the stony circuitous route,
the power of threat women teach,
overgrown, deserted, exposed, like Adam.

The Holiday Inn breakfast special

"I wouldn't recommend this breakfast
to anyone," she says as I search
the menu. He wears an orange shirt
of big brown flowers shirred with orange
plastic buttons. Her face lists
on an eroded lake bed. "Eggs taste
like what they serve on planes. And the pancakes—
horrible!" Eavesdropping I order
the breakfast special and pretend
deafness.
    Sixtyish and seventy, they
have evaporated down to pension,
savings book, a paid-up home. Today
he wears a cowrie necklace—Hawaiian
potency—a ninety-eight cents bargain.
She reads the brochures, ticking off
prices for shows, tours, luaus. What they want
from these late islands can only be bought.
Outdoors the Waikiki waves flaunt
gay boys and honeymooners, fat women
who float by wickedly.
      I wolf down
the rosy yolk, pour maple syrup
on the pancakes, as they leave. *Mahalo
aloha!* She's left her plate untouched
and he no tip for service.

Sexing

Every May the golden flowers spring,
as many as unwanted children,
stretches of sunshine fallen on wasteland,
or cheering intruders on somber lawns.
No one can pick them fast enough,
for that's the nature of weeds, to outdo
demand and sicken desire. Yet there will
always be some to love their spiky single
blossoms, like running stitches radiating
from tightly knotted hearts; and the name
to call them—a common thing turned wonderful
by naming—the dandelions' quirky gaze,
like some summering beasts with yellow pupils
to make your skin feel it's all over you.
                                        I like
their cocky profligacy for the briefest
springtime; then overnight to ashy semen
choking in nose and mouth, in this monstrous
sexing that has nothing to do with me.

Greenhouse effect in New York

Today I wake up and it's
already eighty-two in the shade.
The weathercable bleats:
humidity is near tropical;
dew point set at seventy-eight.
It is too hot for coffee
but I make it anyway.
Steam puffs from the shabby
kettle and not quite
evaporates in the closed
peeling kitchen. I fantasize
fungal jungles devour
the Comet under the sink.
My husband is away in Finland.
He is eating cloudberries
and reindeer steak; he will grow
even more Caucasian cool,
a Slav from remote winters
with a meaty manly texture
evolved for frigid conditions.

My coffee is instant. Its vapor
rises saturated with berries
from Sumatra, whose mountains lie
visible on the sharply strung
horizon of the Malacca Straits:
my Malacca Straits where
it is always eighty-two
and childhood's a fermented
dew point of denials
and tears. I breathe the roasted-
berry smog. It covers my cheeks

with the sweat of plantations,
a brown aroma from Southeast
Asia like sun-dried anchovies
just this side of rotten.
                    This is
my usual heat. I am my
usual self—husbandless for
two weeks—returned to normalcy,
to rain-forest torpor
whose water swells and swells
in cumulus clumps. The sky
rumbles all day and night, like
vague threats a child overhears.
Her unnourished eyelids tremble,
pull down in spite of herself.
She is so hungry that sleep must
fill her full of dew which is wet
but never cool. I drink
the bitter brew. Sugar
is no good for someone like me
who hoards sullen solitudes
against the approaching front.

The anniversary

The world's fullness is gratefully
more than you can admit. The seams
pull taut, crotch aches, armpits peel
back odors like onion layers,
sliding pale skin on pale skin, till
the moisture streams through uterus,
pores, every way out, like smoggy
summer rain. The smells! as tarry sizzles
on blacktop, cement humidity, decayed rinds
of melons, pork butt, soggy lettuce.
You jiggle the fishbone
out of your throat, glad to be alive,
glad for blisters in the voice-box—
glad, naturally, to be keeping score:
pow! take that, old socks, and you, bitch-
death! Even gulls scream as they score
above the garbage scow.
                                        I take up my pen
in pleasure of breaking, which is happening
all over, in horror, in desire, whether
you insist or absent yourself. Praise
life's kisses, massive masseur,
kisses more than you can write: fullness
of words when even bad poets
have footsteps which stick through muck,
sloshing loosely, crippled feet in borrowed
galoshes: fullness of breasts,
their sugary heat dripping from eyes
of nipples, crying for the mouths of innocents,
the unspeaking gummy tongues in mouths
of dangling boys.
                              When the womb
is distended, the glimmering skin stretched

like a moon-curved canvas, a fat
sag of wind: if the tasty fish
jumps to the frying pan, who will blame
it? In the mother's smothering clasp,
the moist powder of her body, he is already
turning away: she is more than he can admit.
She is milk, tears, salt, sugar, vinegar
like opened wine, tart as lime
from the Chinese tropics; she is flesh,
what goes away, despairs, the fullness
of musings and kisses. He will know her
as infinity, victim, cannibal, cymbals,
humming high wires, air of his savoring,
rivers of nutrients, aridity. There
is no integrity in her mothering.
Instead, flow and breaking ocean,
blood, bile, freshly springing
saliva from eyes and yearning.
If I take up my pen in the anniversary
of fullness, if I remember also
another breaking, filaments forced
earthwards, plunged into the uncreated,
if I take up my pen, will I be forgiven?

Mother in the suburbs

Behind the wheel, suddenly still, I wait.
Afternoon September sun sifts and soaks
the blurred glass, the steel and plastic car.
I open my eyes on the quiet lane. A man
hunched in a skin-tight black and yellow
bodysuit is silently pedalling

down the road. Nothing moves while he's pedalling
but himself. I am sinking as I wait
on this amber afternoon for the yellow
bus. The sun's fire burns on the steel and soaks
my skin in leisurely laps, like a man
intently stroking a woman in his car.

I hear a roar of imminent cars,
imagine the cyclist swifter pedalling
in flash-frozen motions, a desperate man
whose bodysuit sweats ambition. I wait;
it is enough to watch the sweat drip and soak
the plastic seat. Soon a towtruck, yellow,

thunders past: I mistake it for the yellow
bus, the aristocratic loaded car
bearing heirlooms. Fear, strong as resin, soaks
the sodden afternoon. My heart's pedalling
minutes up an empty hill as I wait
the first day of separation for a man

driving a bus. I must trust a strange man
high on a single seat in a yellow
bus. Wayside sumac bushes, shivering, wait,
as gold, maroon, and black shining cars
spin by. The autumnal sun is pedalling
through tall Douglas firs whose leathery bark soaks

light as a dry rag on a dish will soak
up moisture, or a woman the fear of a man
in a black and yellow bodysuit pedalling
out of the way of a lumbering yellow
towtruck. No accounting for why these cars
rush from place to place, for why I wait

by the newly planted pines for a man
I don't know who drives so late a yellow
chariot bearing my son for whom I wait.

Tennis

A little piss god, he grips his weapon, hurls
against the yellow ball derailing past.
Three girls in pink sweats and hearts
twang gut and giggle. In the observers' room
a young man cradles his strings. It could be
twenty years later, and I dead from too
much mother love come back to spy
on the Saturday star and his singles partner
trailing on his moves.
                Unseen, I stiffen
in the grosgrained tubular chair, all mother,
asking, who is that woman with you,
her nose unlikable as a fishing blade,
hips like highways, suburban bleached
in health-club whites? The raw hemp of marriage
is wound around her wrist, flies from his racquet,
a tall American god whom I'd raised
to know woman's sacrifice. Cut quick I see
her hearty game, my son's first tennis lesson,
my knotted face in her distracted gaze,
bonds we do when we most think to love
and free. Below, the balls cluster on
the levelled green, not like eggs that break
uncounted generations, but as
taskmasters worrying the initiate:
master me, master me.

Tag sale

It's in Mt. Kisco, New York; Danbury,
Connecticut; Newton, Massachusetts;
or some nameless suburb, California.
The woman sits among card tables
arranged with things. Soiled black-and-white
bleaching to sepia, clothes washed transparent,
trays of plastic disks, glass beads winking
in weekend sunshine—topaz, emerald,
flat blues and pink-skinned faux pearls.
Someone wore them once in some
exciting place. She turns a fat face,
narrow chin sheltered by years of good
living. These are her things. We can have them
for the price sticky-taped to each: the lamp
from Ohio with scaling brassy dragons
an American artisan dreamed as oriental.
Her G.I. husband picked it for a song
for his homesick wife. After twenty years
she has given up explaining it is not
the real thing, will take five dollars for it.
Ditto the cane lounge from Taiwan.
It claimed kin for a generation
in a corner of the tract house.
Everything else is standard American:
ironware, flatware, fiberglass drapes
guaranteed a lifetime; herculean sofa.

The young man stands aside. He will carry
the goods to campers pulled up in the driveway.
Goodbye to strangers. He can't wait for us
to leave. Is she his mother, his furious
expression a son's? Can an American son
hate a Korean mother? Or has he come,
stranger, to a stranger's house?

Here on this plain surface
are her things. She does not want them.

Taking off

Knee by knee, fat chins in chests, cigar tubes of 270s stack like
rolls of quarters from Queens to heaven, waiting for taxiing.

No escape from the fifty year old silver-haired woman with the tea-
room voice who asks the black gentleman for his window seat and
now chats amiably about swordfish steaks and her son's favorite dishes
for the hour we 270 sit on the ground like a squashed cow patty.

The women's salon frizzes uncurl; sighs waft incense of impatience.
Such occidental forbearance. Some read, sheets of newspapers
crackling like breakers over their heartbreak.

Behind me the young West Indian and the silvery woman with the
plumy voice exchange confidences, private details of kitchen and
travel. Their lives unscroll in monotones and beeps.

How calm we are—airless, temperature rising, surrounded by hidden
oxygen masks, yellow life jackets under every bottom. Life cots
provided for baby, we read. Cheerfully we watch the movie where a
blonde shows us how the life jackets come with whistles and lights.

The oily Atlantic ocean surges by Sheepshead Bay with 270
Christmas lights tweeting in the bleak winter night.

Reluctantly the engines boom; wheels thirp and turn into the wind,
down flaring trails behind a line of winged others massive throbbing
into the layered uncanny, and even the courting matron is silent as
we climb, we finally climb into the sky.

Riding into California

If you come to a land with no ancestors
to bless you, you have to be your own
ancestor. The veterans in the mobile home
park don't want to be there. It isn't easy.
Oil rigs litter the land like giant frozen birds.
Ghosts welcome us to a new life, and
an immigrant without home ghosts
cannot believe the land is real. So you're
grateful for familiarity, and Bruce Lee
becomes your hero. Coming into Fullerton,
everyone waiting at the station is white.
The good thing about being Chinese on Amtrack
is no one sits next to you. The bad thing is
you sit alone all the way to Irvine.

The whistler

It's 2 a.m. and I hear a whistle
in Berkeley on Peralta Avenue.
The whistle re-echoes,
so I rise in my thin blue gown
and slip out the door into
the city of notorious memories.
The whistler is a white demon startled
by my appearance on the cold street.
He is surprised at the humanity
summoned by his thin pursed lips.
He has not known himself to be
so powerful, that sharp bright note
of his tonguing capable
of inducing a woman to rise from
her safe bed and approach.
I see he doesn't know what
to do with my presence.
I stand, my bare feet aching
on the pavement powdered
with sweet white alyssum
in its cracks. He doesn't know
whether to ravish me or to kill
me, to crush my breasts and brains
between stones and make a lesson of me,
a no-shame woman who answers a whistle
as abject as a dog, now sorry
for having listened having risen,
having come to a demon whistler
at two in the morning
among the rose leaves spotted with fungus,
hoping for a memory of her own,

and meeting instead a murderer
ghost from a different world,
who hesitates then vanishes
leaving me shivering
with the unweeded yard of a
stranger's home as my witness.

Romancing Bukowski
(After Ginsberg)

Someone said I'd meet you at the awards dinner
among the starched white table cloths on the third floor
of the Los Angeles Athletic Club.
I looked for you between the blooming blue-
and-green paisley carpets and naugahyde club chairs.
I had no idea who you are—short, affable,
with a mobile goatee, or tall, bald, and hunched
from listening down to adoring fans.
I expected you'd be wearing blue jeans and black
turtle-neck, despite the seventy degree
May weather and your reverent age.
We would connect immediately for
I have been looking for someone like you
all my life, the unforgettable casual
California poet who soliloquizes
on what counts and doesn't count.

Afraid to introduce myself, I gaze
at the suited resident masculines.
They may be mass murderers waiting
on the other side of the banquette,
the ones who kill prostitutes, who lure
children, who consume fleshy parts.
A woman outfitted with classy Monet
jewelry and a crafty shawl tells me her friend
has written a biography of Amy Vanderbilt:
what makes her interesting is she was rich.
Thinking of you, I tell her I've never wanted
to be rich.
        I was lying, of course, to make
an impression. That was how the evening went,
Bukowski, because you weren't there.

Strange meeting

Larger than a city block the Boeing wheels
past the LAX viewing glass. Its hollow body
glows with myriad eyes, each eye holding you
gliding into Los Angeles. It is seven years
since we've met, and more than twice seven years
before that. Two babies separate us,
brown boys with different mates. Together
we have managed to pull apart whatever
pushed us together. If you come down that gray
industrial carpet, your rolling shuffle
just the same as that young man's whose
American speech had splintered my native ears,
I will take you home inside myself, a cannibal,
to eat your juicy heart, mingling blood with blood.
Or like that thick-shelled bird, carry you
in my glowing body, howling in the wind-stream,
back to where we both have been. The moment passes,
baffled by love, and what it cannot do.

Huntington Gardens

Inspired by history we walk looking
backwards through the railroad baron's park.
The giant cactus is armored, has swelled
for almost a century. Chicken-
and-eggs and red fleshy stone cacti
crowd by the shredded feet of aloes.

Here is a garden of thorns and mean pricks
where shivering hummingbirds fly in and out
of razor-sharp branches like *raza* in the barrios.

Monarchs flit orange silks across an unblinking
blue eye. We let the gentle midges mumble
to us in distant Buddhist voices, glimpse

in the tangled canopies of surfeited
roses falling petals into which much water
has been poured: plenty, heaped trellis
upon trellis, buzzing with golden bees.

New house

The new house bears marks of families.
A dog's paw lies imprinted on the polished adobe tile.
Some evenings, waiting for my teenage son
to come home, I find it as poignant
as the Pompeii plaster cast corpses displayed
in coffee-table volumes for the well-traveled.
A wall of built-in cupboards hang against the day
when the big one will roll, put up after the
'77 quake broke the family china.
Six palms rattle in a sundowner, lined-up,
shooting for a postcard silhouette.
I would have done none of these, have had to shift
my life to fit them in: traces, residue, strangers'
sticky memories that now must be my own.

Miranda in Santa Barbara

1. The patio

Oleander blossoms crimson and snow
against blue bleached skies.
The furiously palpitating hummingbird
tippling at the fuchsia's open lips
is unconcerned. What can stop
the Pacific's blundering swells
or the hard green orange tits
from coloring? Only she, resisting
the geranium's invitation at this
giant chalkboard of the years, may rise
from naps, from bird-whistle
and the pool's mechanic circulation,
to find her shelter from the senses.

2. The bedroom

Nine! blinks the three-inch hour.
Tuesday night. The turkey burger
was disagreeable. She has never
recovered from being a child, dying
for attention. Me me me me me.
Where's Father? Where's Mother? Baby
lives in California now. No one is dying.

Again she trots to the bathroom—
irritable bowels. The night has hardly begun.
It's already orphan grim.
The inexorable numbers pulse. Yes.

Clocks have a way of pushing free
of whatever holds back. Regrets,
sorrow. She doses
herself firmly with Pepto-Bismol:
father pink bottle, mother spoon.
Sends herself off to bed, growing up small.

3. Stern's Wharf

The mix of pheromones, fresh ozone
from a Pacific indigo,
reflecting vastnesses, nervous
bodies jostling volley balls
in the calm glittering air.
Miranda gazes at their pink flesh,
stammering muscles. Who is alien,
who at home? Ironical
she spends her days like coins,
on edge for the bandit clatter:
a spill of silver lit
by expectation, with the cyclists,
the rollerbladders and runners,
with the winey homeless and tourists.

4. Cottage Hospital

The sun sinking behind linen drapes,
and the irises, avid, giant-lipped,
gasping at stale water, light,
are already dead, with only the pallor ·
of beauty cast above the rayon ribbons.
No, this is not her world, although it is,
for the moment, the figure on the mantel,
emblazoned in crepuscular folds,
that picks its twin like a sharpshooter.

The breakers roll over the dry brown sand,
over a woman's face, sixty, folded
in creases, frantic for beauty.
Beside her, the stalky child, ready
for his spring into manhood.
Miranda refuses these twin dancing figures,
crying like the irises, more light, more light.

Learning to love America

because it has no pure products

because the Pacific Ocean sweeps along the coastline
because the water of the ocean is cold
and because land is better than ocean

because I say we rather than they

because I live in California
I have eaten fresh artichokes
and jacarandas bloom in April and May

because my senses have caught up with my body
my breath with the air it swallows
my hunger with my mouth

because I walk barefoot in my house

because I have nursed my son at my breast
because he is a strong American boy
because I have seen his eyes redden when he is asked who he is
because he answers I don't know

because to have a son is to have a country
because my son will bury me here
because countries are in our blood and we bleed them

because it is late and too late to change my mind
because it is time.

Starry night

He could always find Orion;
although young
he saw the innocent sword.

Because I was his mother
I could not speak what boys
should know. No sharing of manhood

between us. I keep silence
before the faintly moving stars.

Monarchs steering

Burnt sienna and sun they lie
on the sharp white petals submerged
in floral light. Arrived after three months
crossing from the bitter alcoholic milksaps
east to the Pacific where oranges brightly
palpitate to an orgasmic infusion.
One stops on an oleander leaf-tip,
another lifts off into warm oxygen,
and yet another luminescent pilot.
Two yards over a pair dallies.
Morning signals the passing Monarchs,
taking my eye, like silent flirts, like women,
after long journeying, taking to scent and heat.
I steer, to the years' indirection.

In California with Neruda

I.

Cockeyed Neruda dancing on a strobe
  of a thousand angels didn't ask
    about angels but for a drink of water.
Be my angel, my fat Chilean, stroke
  feathery breath, imploding pulse, wake me
    to the chaparral beneath the skin, the Pacific–
thundering surf inside my eyes. Oh come
to California and stand with me as earth
  coughs, rifts shimmer, adobe cathedrals cracking open
    roll like dice. Wise man of the Americas,
make a wise woman out of me. Seize
  my lines and do not let go, for death
    is not yet to be written in this new-found land,
foreclosing forms and poetry ended.

II.

    When the grey watery air sifts through Santa Barbara
like flour in a pan, wholesome, light, changing element
to nutrient, and when between the swirling marine layers
the green ribs of palms sway, ticklish in early morning,
it is not yet three but already my angel is walking,
striking at old manzanita with his cane, his panama
hat cocked to his brow.
          Indoors the refrigerator clicks and groans,
an old lady mashing her cereal. He has no liking for crones,
departs through the colored glass door impatiently
(he is not deceived by decoration: a door is a door,
whether steel or glass). The street lamps pace him.
Bare bony structures with bright obscene noses,
they tell him about darkness visible, whose neighbors'
brown roses have shrunk into fall's clammy fists.

III.

Not so fast, dear Pablo Neruda! The suburban tracts
sleep while you shuttle, but not the tossing khaki eucalyptus
or many-leafed olive trees guarding black messy feet.
The white undersides of rosemary flash by a pink wall,
oranges beckon like globed neons in run-down diners.
Lusty lavender spikes crust the tall bushes.
I pinch them, scented fingers; crumble them in my pocket,
sneezing, sinuses backed up, while you stride ahead
undisturbed by common colds, pollen, identities, all longings
of the middle-class and the female kind. Can you smell
the copper of menstrual overflows on my breath, and what
do you make of it in the murky California streetlight
before ambitious ignition keys jump-start the day?

IV.

Neruda, did you know history? Or did you live it,
    one day at a time, through the clichés of revolution
        and boring justifications? Crossing the green belt you glance
down at the creek, withered by August, its March
    impetuosity commemorated by upturned oaks
        and swathed sandy shoulders. Now its water
trickles a bathtub melody even a dog can step over
    with dry paws. These details do not detain you
        for poetry is larger than a September creek in suburbia.
You are determined to walk your nine miles,
    nine the shaman's number called up by association.
    "And that too is history," you murmur. "There is no poetry
but association, no history but poetry, which we swallow
with fresh eggs in the morning, one after the other."

V.

Nothing but contingency, a line of spermatozoa,
the body, the vulva, flexing to its heartbeat,
and words, a pure rhythm of naming one sensation
after another?
                    Is this why you get me up in the mornings,
angelic poet, to walk around and around?
Naming the traffic, the malls, the boys in their uniforms
    of defense and desire, women smoky with hurt
        making sandwiches for school lunches,
Indians chanting through pow-wows, Koreans hymning:
    the entire looping litany of the 49th parallel—
        blacks, whites, Jews, Latinos, Asians,
jamming Los Angeles and Disneyland, the continental
contingency of California breaking out
even as we hurry across driveways in the blink before sunrise.

Oranges

He comes into sight, a fading tee-shirt,
offering a sack of navels
as my car shakes where the traffic lights
are changing, their amber globes
glittering like neon. The lights
jump from red to green
in minutes, too quick for a sale.
On the median in the sunshine
he stands with a bunch of webbed
bags stuffed with oranges, a bounty visible
all over Southern California,
on trees heavily loaded
with fruit, thousands on thousands,
like the fabled Spanish galleons
sailing over the Atlantic,
bearing ingots to despoil Europe.
His fingers signal: one bag for five dollars.
I imagine their sour taste watering
my mouth—the acid harvest of field hands.
A peddler, he does not care
about supermarkets, take-outs,
and factories manufacturing
frozen orange juice. He has arrived
from a field of open furrows
and malathion sprays,
from sleeping in a lean-to
under the Los Angeles freeway
beside a river of concrete. The waves
of automobiles do not shock him.

They no longer terrify. The June
heat is saturated with petroleum fumes,
but he smells the scent of his life
under these emissions—sweat, hunger,
his male eagerness for night.
He is alone on the narrow island,
alone with the eddying
jaguars, cougars, and broncos,
enveloped in the taste of strange names:
Toyotas, Fords, Hondas,
Subarus and Volvos,
Volkswagen and Cadillac.
His feet are snagged in sacks
of oranges, the dream of oranges
now stale, stagnant, while he waits
for the cool night to spring
him from the noisy pulsing intricate
intersection, but still bright
as the oranges left glowing on trees
in orchards, the fenced plots and gardens
in the backyards of America.

Self-portrait

I want to write a self-portrait
like Rosario Castellanos
who knew herself so well
she could knife herself in the back
and laugh. She knew how she
appeared to the world, her desire
awry like a misplaced wig.
But I cannot see myself.
My eye is mercurial.
I flake, the particulars
drizzling with deformations.
I know how to be happy
but lack the means.
Unlike my friend Rosario
my skin is thin. Inside its bag
are late-night monsters
impossible to describe.
They watch even as my green-
stem son eats noodle soup.
I have more desires than
there are wigs in the world:
to be what I am not.
Also to be myself. To speak
many languages, each
as useful as this one
I wipe my tears with.
I want to be good and better
than I am. I want to sway
like the swaying palms
and hold heavy books in my hands.

Shirley Geok-lin Lim was born in the historic British colony of Malacca, Malaysia, and her work reflects both her Chinese-Malaysian heritage and the social and literary landscape of the United States of which she is now a citizen. Arriving in Boston in 1969, she studied with J. V. Cunningham, to whom she dedicated her Commonwealth Prize-winning first book of poems, *Crossing the Peninsula* (Heinemann, 1980). Anthologized as both an Asian and an Asian-American author, Lim received a Ph.D. in English and American Literature from Brandeis University and is currently professor of English and Women's Studies at the University of California, Santa Barbara, and Chair of Women's Studies. She remains an observer of Southeast Asian life, retaining important links to the Pacific Rim's literary community, even as she is gaining an identity as a California writer. Author of four books of poetry, three collections of stories, and two critical books, she received the American Book Award for her recent memoir, *Among the White Moon Faces* (1996, Feminist Press). Among her many edited and co-edited volumes, the anthology, *The Forbidden Stitch: An Asian American Women's Anthology,* received the American Book Award in 1990. She has been the recipient of numerous other awards, including teaching awards, National Endowment for the Humanities Summer Awards, and a Fulbright Distinguished Lecturer Award in 1996.